Who Knew?

25 Quizzes to
Help You Find
Your Secret Self

by Beth Mayall

SCHOLASTIC INC.
New York Toronto London Auckland Sydney
Mexico City New Delhi Hong Kong

For my family and Drew.
And for all my
All About You chicks.

Cover photos by Jon McKee.

Design by Louise Bova

ISBN 0-439-16139-8

12 11 10 9 8 7 6 5 4 3 2 1   1 2 3 4 5 6/0

Printed in the U.S.A.   01

First Scholastic Trade paperback printing, April 2001

Contents

Introduction
The Real You

You know how people change? Like, when you go away for the summer and come back to school three months later — and barely recognize some of your best buds? Maybe they look different. Or sound different. Or maybe they just give off a more mature vibe that makes you feel like you have to get to know them all over again. It can be pretty freaky when someone you know changes in a big way.

But here's another freaky thing: The same kind of changes could be happening to you. Right now.

The quizzes in this book will help you realize the changes you're going through. By the end, you'll understand lots about yourself and the new you — from the reasons your friends confide in you to how creative you are . . . and, of course, almost everything in between.

So are you ready to discover your secret self? Then flip the page and get going.

Chapter One

The Secret You

Discover the cool chick inside you!

OK, so you're always growing and changing — but deep inside there's a rock-solid YOU. Find out more about your true, unique, sometimes-hidden self with these quizzes!

WHO'S THE REAL YOU?

Do you hide behind a wall of little white lies, or do you let people hear all your innermost thoughts — even the harsh ones? Circle the letter that sounds most like what you would do in a given situation.

1. *Awww!* Grandma has spent every Sunday for a month knitting you a very special sweater. You open the box on the night of the big family din-

ner and see this fluffy, hideous polka-dot thing that would fit you — and three of your friends! What's your reaction?

a) Hug her and tell her how cool it is.

X b) Point out something you like about the sweater, like the fact that it's a turtleneck. Then you decide you'll wear it once or twice — when she comes to visit.

c) Mention that it's big and *very* polka-dotty.

2. Your friend's new haircut looks like your kid sister did it — in the dark! She asks if you like it. You take a deeeeep breath and say:

a) "Are you kidding? I *love* it!" Once it grows out, you might tell her your real feelings but not now.

b) "Um, you should demand a refund from that salon." A true friend wouldn't let her walk around looking like that!

X c) "It's really different from your old look. How do *you* like it?" Then offer some style suggestions if she's unhappy with it.

3. You sell candy bars for two months to help your music class raise money for underprivileged kids. The grand total is $500 and you are psyched, but some classmates start talking

about using the money for a "field trip" to a Britney Spears concert instead. What's your move?

a) Suggest that the class take a vote — and remind everybody that the kids were really counting on this money.

b) Tell them that you're totally disgusted! How can they be so selfish and mean?

c) Let them decide how to spend the cash. You'll go along with whatever everybody else wants.

4. Your partner did absolutely *no* work on the mini volcano you supposedly built as a "team" project. When you get an A+ and the teacher asks *him* to do a demonstration for your science class, you:

a) slouch down in your seat and roll your eyes but don't make a big deal out of it.

b) yell out, "But I did all the work!"

c) raise your hand and ask if you can do the demonstration together — after all, you *are* partners, right? You deserve at least half the glory.

5. A nerdy kid two grades younger than you is getting teased by a group of bullies in the school playground. What do you do?

a) Start teasing the bullies by saying, "Ooh! You're so tough picking on a kid two years younger than you — how cool!" and push them around. They deserve to be picked on after being so mean.

b) Walk on by — it's none of your business.

c) Walk up and say, "Hey, what's the problem here?" to the meanies. Tell them if you see this happening again, you'll report them to their teacher.

SCORING:

Add up your points and read the scoring section below.

1. a=1, b=2, c=3
2. a=1, b=3, c=2
3. a=2, b=3, c=1
4. a=1, b=3, c=2
5. a=3, b=1, c=2

YOUR TOTAL: _____

If you scored 12 to 15 . . . Say It Like It Is
You get a big ole "Go, girl!" for your ability to speak your mind. Most people have a tough time getting up the nerve to say exactly what they're thinking. But that isn't a prob for you! You're an

assertive girl who says what's on her mind. One thing to think about: Could you sometimes be a little *too* honest — like, to the point that you hurt people's feelings with your brutal openness? You might want to tone it down sometimes.

If you scored 8 to 11 . . . The Perfect-o Balance
You're more well-balanced than most grown-ups. What's it mean? Well, you know that sometimes life's toughest moments call for a teensy bending of the rules. (No need to hurt people's feelings, right?) But most of the time, your motto is: Treat others as you would like to be treated — fairly and honestly. And that seems to work just great!

If you scored 5 to 7 . . . The Conflict Avoider
You hate drawing attention to yourself, don'tcha? But you really need to make your voice heard more often! By not making choices (or white-lying your way out of awkward situations to avoid confrontation), you're selling yourself *way* short. C'mon — you have opinions! Let people hear 'em. Start small — like by telling friends what movie *you'd* like to see for once. The people you love and respect deserve to know the real you. And what about white lies? It depends. When it comes to sparing somebody's feelings by softening the truth, that's usually OK. But if you do it all the time (and let white lies turn into full-fledged un-

truths!), you'll end up feeling bad and dishonest. Instead of telling people what you think they wanna hear, try to speak your mind.

******

ARE YOU TOO SHY?

Sure — everybody says, "Just be yourself" and you'll make friends. But that's kind of tough when you're freaked out by the idea of talking to new people! So are you outgoing enough? Answer true or false to the following scenarios and find out.

1. You'll raise your hand in class if you're positive you know the answer.

2. You'll raise your hand if you're 50 percent sure you know the answer.

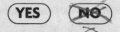

3. If you're seated next to the new girl in class, you'll introduce yourself.

4. If you're seated next to the new boy in class, you'll introduce yourself.

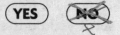

5. Your school has the *number one* softball team

in the district — and that happens to be your best sport. When you look at the sign-up sheet for tryouts, you see that it's filled with the names of all the coolest girls in your school. You would add your name to the list in a heartbeat.

6. At a family barbecue, all your older cousins are roasting marshmallows and telling jokes. You heard a great one on the radio this morning, so when there's an open spot in the conversation, you jump in to tell yours.

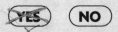

7. While you and your friends are out riding bikes, you get totally and completely lost. You come to a gas station in the middle of nowhere and your friends beg you to go ask for directions while they guard the bikes. You say OK and do it — it's no big deal.

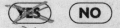

8. A new family moves in down the street. You go over there as soon as you see the moving van pull up, excited to introduce yourself.

9. For your basketball team fund-raiser, you have to sell 25 raffle tickets. You're comfy going

to the mall food court and bugging the kids who
hang there to buy 'em.

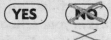

YES   NO

SCORING:

*Give yourself three points for each yes answer and
one point for each no answer.*

YOUR TOTAL: 12 2✗

If you scored 21 to 27 . . . The Life of the Party
You're one outspoken gal. It's cool that you aren't
intimidated by people — even strangers or big
groups. Ever think about joining the debate team
when you get to high school? Open, friendly
people like you make awesome public speak-
ers . . . and stand-up comedians!

If you scored 14 to 20 . . . Partly Partyin'
You aren't the girl who always has everyone's attention at lunch . . . but you aren't hiding under-
neath the table, either. Sometimes you take
risks — like by being extra-friendly or extra-
goofy — but not all the time! One thing to think
about: Know that rush you feel when you shed
your shyness? With some work, you could feel
that happy buzz a whole lot more often!

If you scored 9 to 13 . . . Party of One

Hello, mellow chick! Ever feel like you're blending into the wallpaper? OK, so it's pretty common for girls your age to be shy — but life's more fun when you break outta that shell! And once you take a risk to make new friends, you might find that you believe in yourself a whole lot more. Read on for tips on how to be more outgoing.

SIX SUREFIRE CONVERSATION STARTERS YOU CAN USE!

1. **Get plugged in.** Ask a classmate for her opinion on stuff you heard on the radio or saw on TV. Or ask her if she's seen any good movies lately.

2. **Get an open-ended question going.** To start a chat, avoid questions that can be answered with a simple "yes" or "no," like: "Isn't this school pizza disgusting?" Instead, go a little deeper, like: "*Why* do you think school pizza is so disgusting?" so the convo doesn't end immediately.

3. **Get observant.** Notice other kids' book covers and backpacks. Do they show a band? A sports team? Or is she carrying a musical instrument around? That's perfect stuff to ask questions about! "What's their new CD like?" "How many games have you gone to?" "How long have you played the tuba?"

4. **Get curious.** Go ahead and ask for advice when you

have a problem. "How did you outline that chapter?" "I'm so confused — what is this book about, anyway?"

5. Get thinkin' out loud. Is your classroom hotter than, um, all five Backstreet Boys? Is there a weird smell in the room? Is the slide presentation so boring that you're almost falling asleep? Share your thoughts with a friendly face nearby. It's a great way to be approachable.

6. Get good ears. Not many people are truly great listeners — but you could be one of the few. Use the chat-starters listed above and then *really* listen to people's answers. You'll be surprised how quickly good questions pop into your mind when you're really listening to what the other person is saying.

******

WHAT'S YOUR SECRET ADMIRER STYLE?

When it comes to boys, do you want everyone (including your crush) to know who you have your eye on or would you prefer to keep it to yourself, thank you very much? Start with question one, then follow the directions next to the answer you choose for which question to jump to next.

1. If you like a boy, you'll send him a note — with your name on it!

> true → *go to question two*
>
> false → *go to question three*

2. Your note would mostly mention:

How cute he is! → *go to question four*

How nice or smart he is! → *go to question five*

3. You'd rather have your best friend do the love-connection work for you.

Yup, that's what best friends do for each other! → *go to question six*

X (No,) you'll do it yourself — eventually! → *go to question five*

4. You usually tell a bunch of people who you have a crush on.

true → *go to question seven*

false → *go to question eight*

5. If it turned out that your Romeo wasn't crushing back, would you still want to be friends?

X (Yeah,) he's a cool boy to have around. → *go to question eight*

(No) way! I'd be too embarrassed! → *go to question seven*

6. Would your secret admirer note be more than one page long?

Yes, I have lots to say! → *go to question eight*

No — he might figure out who I am! → *go to question nine*

7. If all of a sudden you got a secret admirer note, what would you do?

Study his handwriting with a few friends to see if you can figure out who he is. → *go to Scoring Section One*

Practically float on a cloud all day, you'd be so happy! But you wouldn't tell many friends. → *go to question eight*

8. You've sent a boy secret admirer notes every day for three weeks. If he came up to you after school (alone!) and asked if it was you, you would:

Tell the truth! → *go to Scoring Section Two*

Lie, lie, and lie some more! No way you'd tell! → *go to Scoring Section Three*

9. Whoopee! You're on the same team with him in gym class. The game? Dodgeball — your *best* sport! How would you play that day?

Very well — as always! → *go to Scoring Section Two*

Terribly! You're so nervous that you can't even aim. → *go to Scoring Section Three*

SCORING SECTION ONE:

Dear Not-so-secret Admirer . . .

Welcome to Obsession Land! When you develop a crush on someone, you tell the world! The good news is that sometimes this method works to your advantage. When the boy hears about your feelings, he may come running! The bad news? By letting your secret out so early, the rumor spreads before you even figure out whether you really like this boy. Our advice? Before you declare who your crush is, take time to figure out whether you even *like* him first!

SCORING SECTION TWO:

Dear Expert Admirer . . .

Congrats! You have this whole secret admirer thing under control. What gets you interested in a boy isn't shallow stuff like looks or clothes or popularity — it's all about his personality. For the most part you're pretty quiet when you're crushin' on somebody. You like being cautious 'cause you'd *die* if your crush laughed in your face. But once you get to know him and you're sure he's super nice, you'll tell a few friends. You've got all the right moves!

Dear Not Interested . . .

Looks like you're kinda freaked by the idea of letting your crush turn into anything more — and that's totally fine. While you're probably chatty and funny with friends, you freeze up when a boy is around — especially one you like! For now, enjoy hangin' with your gal pals. Hang out. Laugh. Relax. The boys can come later. No rush.

******

DO YOU WHINE TOO MUCH?

Yeah, you definitely should speak up when something really bugs you — but do you complain *all* the time? Or maybe you're like a human doormat, letting people walk all over you 24/7. Find out if people are just about sick of your "poor me!" talk by circling the letter that sounds most like how you would react to these situations.

1. Your school is considering starting a dress code — girls in skirts, guys in ties! You see a girl with an anti-dress-code petition in the caf, so you walk up to her and:

a) ask to sign it.

b) ask if you can help by starting another petition.

16

c) say, "It's no use fighting the dress-code thing. It's gonna happen if they want it to."

2. The role of Juliet was practically *made* for you — but, unfortunately the drama teacher doesn't agree. She casts you as the nurse instead. Your reaction?

a) You're psyched just to be in the play! And the nurse's part is actually pretty cool.

b) Beg the drama teacher to let you try out for Juliet again, since you know the lines better now and you're a little less nervous. But there is *no* way you're playing the nurse!

c) After a bit of serious bummin', you're OK. You vow to practice your acting more often so you'll get the lead in the next play.

3. Aloha! Your neighbors have twin babies, and they're going on vacation to Hawaii — and bringing your sister along so she can baby-sit while they swim. What do you do?

a) Tell the neighbors about the time your sister forgot to feed the cat for three days — it almost died! It isn't fair that she gets to go, so you try to mess it up.

b) Tell your sister how jealous you are, and call dibs on the next tropical-island baby-sitting gig.

c) Lend your sister your favorite bathing suit and tell her you're so happy for her.

4. Your best friend's family lets you tag along to a really fancy restaurant. When you open the menu, you see that *every*thing is seafood — which you totally hate! The prob is, you're starving. How do you get through the meal?

a) Order a salad and say you really aren't that hungry.

b) Tell them that you don't eat seafood — it's up to them to figure out something un-fishy for you to eat.

✗ c) Order fried shrimp and just eat the fries and vegetables that come with it instead.

5. It's that once-a-year family dinner night at Great-aunt Edna's — ugh! Looks like a night of getting your cheeks pinched and hearing stories from people who "changed your diaper when you were an itty-bitty baby!" Pure torture. Plus, you have a nasty cold. You:

a) go to dinner because you don't get a chance to see these relatives much, but bow out before the cheek-pinching starts, saying you need to rest.

b) sniffle, sneeze, and cough — but you go to Great-aunt Edna's and hang in there.

✗ c) tell your parents that they can't possibly

expect you to go out when you're feeling like this!

Count up your points and read your scoring section below.

1. a=2, b=3, c=1   2
2. a=3, b=1, c=2   2   2
3. a=1, b=2, c=3   2   1
4. a=3, b=1, c=2   2   2
5. a=2, b=3, c=1   1   1

YOUR TOTAL: _8_   8

If you scored 5 to 7 . . . But What about Me?
You win the Complainer of the Year Award! OK, so it's great to express your thoughts and feelings, but if you only do it when you're unhappy, you sound like a whiner! Make sure you let people know when they do something nice or cool. You're a hard girl to please, and unless you start saying, "Thanks" more often, people might stop doing nice stuff for you. Wouldn't that be too bad?

If you scored 8 to 11 . . . Just about Right
You know how to make the most out of bad situations, and you don't put up with less than you

deserve. You don't make a big deal if things don't turn out your way. But here's the superneat thing: You learn from your mistakes! So even though you might not get first prize on your first try, you will probably get it next time around.

If you scored 12 to 15 . . . All about Denial
You're such a sweetie — never causin' trouble, always smilin', and doin' what you're supposed to do . . . but doesn't that stink sometimes? The truth is, sometimes it's OK to say you're unhappy — even if you're just telling your diary or your best friend. It helps you remember to avoid that situation next time, or to push yourself to work harder to achieve what you want. Don't settle for second-best all the time!
*****

ARE YOU TOO EASILY EMBARRASSED?

Could you fall off the stage during choir rehearsal and laugh it off? Or do you practically turn purple with humiliation at even the littlest mistake? Grade each of the following situations with a one, two, or three to find out.

KEY:

1=Totally humiliating!
2=Kind of embarrassing
3=Not a big deal

_2_ 1. You fall asleep during a movie and when the lights come up, your friends tell you that you were snoring through the last half hour of the flick.

_3_ 2. Mom makes you dress up as a clown (*and* wear a big red nose) for your baby bro's birthday party.

_3_ 3. You hit the bathroom before school starts and, as you're walking to your classroom afterward, a boy coming toward you looks down and cracks up — a huge piece of toilet paper is stuck to your shoe, trailing behind you.

_2_ 4. In your first class of the morning, the kids around you smell something terrible. After searching around, everybody realizes that it's coming from your shoe — you stepped in dog poop! Ew!

_2_ 5. Your mom writes a note on your napkin and sticks it in your lunch bag. You pull it out in the crowded cafeteria and your whole table sees *I love you, sweetie-bear!*

6. Dad follows you into a girls' clothing store and tries on all the hats, just to be a goofball. You see a group of girls from your school cracking up at him.

7. Your health teacher makes you do a speech on puberty — and your class is coed!

8. Your family takes you out to dinner for your birthday and, at the end of the meal, all the waiters and waitresses surround your table, singing "Happy Birthday" to you. (They even make you wear a birthday hat!)

9. In gym class, you're the last one to get picked for the volleyball team.

10. During a test, when the classroom is totally and completely quiet, your stomach growls *really* loudly. Even your teacher looks up at you.

SCORING:

Total the numbers you wrote in slots one through ten and read your answer section below.

YOUR TOTAL: _____

If you scored 25 to 30 . . . Gutsy Girl
You could drop a plate of spaghetti in your lap in front of your crush and you wouldn't even turn pink! Being this bold and fearless is a rare, cool trait. You're self-confident — and probably a little bit of a show-off? Just make sure you aren't hogging *all* the attention.

If you scored 17 to 24 . . . Part-time Pink-faced
You've landed right in the middle of Embarrassment Land. You're in the majority of people who are able to laugh at little embarrassments and turn red at the biggies. So our advice is: Keep doin' what you're doing. As you get older, you'll probably get closer to the Gutsy Girlie above, since you'll learn that just lookin' like a fool doesn't actually *make* you one.

If you scored 10 to 16 . . . Chicken Chick
Most of the things you get red-faced about aren't worth the worry. Most of the time, when you're convinced everyone is watching you and laughing, they're really too focused on their own bad hair days, embarrassing moms, and everything else to even notice you! The bottom line? It's time to ease up, girlfriend, and learn to *laugh* at yourself a little!

Chapter Two

The Homey You

All about hangin' out.

Count up all the hours in the day and how you spend them and you'll see that you pass a lot of 'em hangin' at your home! What you choose to do while you're there says a whole lot about you.

WHAT IS YOUR SLEEPING STYLE?

Can you snooze through marching band practice? Find out if you sleep very lightly or deeper than deep, and discover ways to improve your nightly zzz's. Answer question one, then follow the instructions next to the answer you choose about which question to go to next.

1. What does the noise factor have to be like in order for you to fall asleep?

X O It's okay if the TV or radio is on — background noise doesn't bother me. → *go to question three*

I need total silence. → *go to question two*

2. Do you wake up at even the slightest noise?

yes → *go to question six*

no → *go to question three*

3. Do you usually wake up in the same position you fall asleep in?

yes → *go to question four*

X no → *go to question five*

4. Have you ever fallen asleep during a really boring class?

yes → *go to question seven*

no → *go to question eight*

5. How often do you sleep through the alarm clock's annoying buzz or hit the snooze alarm?

a lot of times → *go to question four*

X rarely or never → *go to question six*

6. Do you frequently wake up in the middle of the night 'cause, um, nature is calling?

yes → *go to question nine*

X no → *go to question eight*

7. Does your sib or your mom often tell you that you talk in your sleep?

> yes → *go to Scoring Section One*
>
> no, or only every once in a while → *go to question eight*

8. How do you feel after taking a fifteen-minute nap?

> (Totally energized!) → *go to question ten*
>
> Totally cheated! → *go to Scoring Section One*

9. Do you hafta have a certain pillow, stuffed animal, or blanket to fall asleep?

> yes → *go to Scoring Section Three*
>
> no → *go to question eight*

10. After a sleepover at your best friend's house, do you usually feel like you got a good night's sleep?

> sorta → *go to Scoring Section Two*
>
> not really → *go to Scoring Section Three*

SCORING SECTION ONE:

Your snooze style: Deep sleeper

   Nighttime must-have: At least eight hours of zzz's — more on weekends!

Sleep pet peeve: Morning people are *so* annoying! It takes you a while to ease into the day — but you're usually fully awake by, like, noon.

To make your sleepy-time even sweeter: Avoid staying up late when you hafta wake up early.

Face facts: Deeeep sleepers like you *need* eight hours of sleep if you wanna be bright and sun-shiny the next day. So give up that extra hour of TV at night and go to bed instead!

(SCORING SECTION TWO:)

Your snooze style: Normal napper

Nighttime must-have: You need to be happy or mellow to fall into a dreamy sleep, so if you're stressed over (oops!) unfinished homework or a fight with a friend, you have trouble catchin' zzz's.

Sleep pet peeve: Sometimes you have a hard time getting to sleep 'cause you're so busy thinking about stuff. You can't turn your brain off, and it keeps you awake!

To make your sleepy-time even sweeter: Check out a tape of oh-so-relaxing nature sounds, like waves crashing or wind blowing, and play it as you fall asleep. It'll help you relax.

SCORING SECTION THREE:

Your snooze style: Restless sleeper

Nighttime must-have: Quiet. Lots of it!

Sleep pet peeve: People who snore, clocks that tick loudly, car alarms that go off in the middle of the night — they all keep you awake!

To make your sleepy-time even sweeter: Ask Mom to buy you an eye mask — a black one that blocks out light. And invest in some neato earplugs. That'll help you fall asleep even when the conditions aren't totally perfect!

WHAT YOUR SLEEPING POSITION REVEALS ABOUT YOUR PERSONALITY

If you sleep . . .

tightly curled up on your side: You need some major love and attention! You're cravin' security — kinda like a baby in its mommy's womb.

stretched out on your side: This is the most common sleeping position, and it means you're way mellow and don't like to fight with people.

on your belly: Sleeping this way makes you feel private and in control — and since it isn't easy to move from this position into another one, it means you aren't a big fan of change. Not being very changeable can also mean that you are very focused — and this is a quality most great leaders have!

on your back: Hel-*lo*! You love being the center of attention. And with huge doses of confidence and charm like you have, you're the life of the party and you make friends easily.

*****

HOW CAN YOU GET YOUR PARENTS TO CHILL OUT?

Here's a cool secret: When Mom and Dad are happy, it makes your life way easier. So what is it they want from you — some peace and quiet? Or some bonding time? Circle the letter that sounds most like you or your situation in each Q and find out what you can do to get your parents to relax.

1. What's the noise level like at your house on weeknights?

    a) Superquiet — it's like livin' in the library!

    b) It's way loud, like a wrestling match.

    c) Pretty light — you can usually hear the TV or someone chatting but there's no major ruckus.

2. Most parents bug their kids over and over about one certain thing. If you had to pick one,

which of these comments is most likely to come out of their mouths?

a) "Why is this place such a mess?"

b) "You're never home anymore! Let's sit down and talk."

c) "Go play in your room — I need some peace and quiet."

3. Check off *all* the following statements that apply to you.

____ a) I fight a little with my siblings. (OK, a lot.)

_✓_ b) My parents are the ones who feed and clean up after the pets.

_✓_ c) It's up to my parents to figure out what's for dinner every night, set the table, and wash the dishes.

____ d) I've hardly spoken to my parents at all lately because I've been so busy with activities and I spend all my free time with friends.

4. How much time do you spend in the same room with your family every day?

a) As much as possible — we're practically attached at the hip!

✗ b) Sometimes half an hour, sometimes an hour or more.

c) Ten minutes or less!

5. Check off all the things that your parents do at least three times a week:

✓ a) Wake you up for school.

✓ b) Ask you about your day.

✓ c) Remind you to do a certain chore — you keep forgetting!

___ d) Ask you to close your bedroom door because you're being too loud.

___ e) Ask you where you've been, because they've been worried.

SCORING:

Add up your points and read your scoring section below.

1) a=15, b=5, c=10   10   20
2) a=10, b=15, c=5   10   10
3) a=5, b=10, c=10, d=15 10   15
4) a=5, b=10, c=15   5   10
5) a=5, b=15, c=10, d=5, e=15 30   15
YOUR TOTAL: 80   10
            75   75

31

If your score was 25 to 50 . . . Get Responsible!

Looks like lots of the 'rents' time is spent taking care of you. And yeah — that *is* part of their job, but it's also time for you to take on some grown-up responsibilities. (Worry not — eventually it gets kinda fun.)

Five easy ways to make your parents happy:

1. Solve fights with your sibs — without Mom's help.

2. After dinner, tell 'em you'll clean up the kitchen so they can go do parent-y stuff.

3. When you have friends over, hang in your bedroom instead of the living room.

4. Set your alarm clock ten minutes earlier in the morning; then you can hit the snooze bar (once!) and still get up on time.

5. Remember this fact: You can blast your stereo without driving everyone crazy by using headphones!

If your score was 55 to 80 . . . Get Workin'!

Seems like you might not be picking up a fair chunk o' chores! Want grumpy parents? Then keep doin' what you're doin'. If, however, you're a smart chickadee who wants Mom and Dad to chill out and stop treating you like a little kid, try some of these easy fix-its.

Five easy ways to make your parents happy:

1. Know that one thing they bug you about over and over (sitting up straight, chewing with your mouth closed, making your bed, or whatever)? Fix it. They'll be happy and more likely to overlook your other, more minor mess-ups!

2. Without being asked, clean up a messy part of the house. Then wait for them to notice.

3. Stop leaving dirty dishes in the sink. Either wash them or put them in the dishwasher.

4. Keep your dirty clothes in a hamper instead of on the bed . . . or the floor . . . or leaving them on the stairs. . . . (You get the idea.)

5. Try making dinner for the family. (You can find kid-friendly recipes on the Web — just type "recipes for kids" into any search engine.) Even if it's not that great, they'll be impressed that you tried.

If your score was 85 to 135 . . . Get Bonding!
Your prob is *easy* to fix! (Lucky girl.) Your parents just want to see more of you — hey, who can blame them? We aren't suggesting that you cling to Mom and Dad like glue; just don't leave the room so quickly that you leave a trail of smoke!

Five easy ways to make your parents happy:

1. If it isn't distracting, do your homework in the same room where your parents are hangin' out after work.

2. Avoid one-word answers to their questions. Like, if they ask how your day went, tell them about something that happened instead of just saying, "Fine!"

3. Show them your test papers and homework assignments — make them feel like they know what's going on in your life.

4. Instead of hanging at the mall or your friend's house, invite your friends to come over to your house once in a while.

5. Here's something that'll shock 'em: Ask Mom how *her* day was. Then stick around long enough to hear the answer!

*****

WHAT'S YOUR MUNCHING STYLE?

Are you a junk-food junkie or a veggie lover? Find your food personality, then try the cool recipe that suits you at the end of your scoring section. Answer question one, then follow the instructions next to the answer you choose about which question to go to next.

1. Do you munch while you watch TV, read, or talk on the phone?

        All the time! → *go to question two*

  X (Not usually.) → *go to question three*

2. Do you frequently find a bag of chips or candy you were munching on suddenly empty?

        Yup — it's like they disappear! → *go to question six*

  X Nope. → *go to question five*

3. Do you eat fresh fruit every day? (Psst — blueberry Pop-Tarts don't count!)

        (yes) → *go to question four*

    x no → *go to question two*

4. Do you sometimes forget to eat during the day?

        Yes, when I'm busy or stressed. → *go to question five*

        (No,) I always remember. → *go to question eight*

5. Do you skip meals (like breakfast) a lot?

        yes → *go to question six*

    x no → *go to question eight*

6. When you and your friends hang out after school, do you ever eat fast food?

       Yup, Taco Bell is my best friend! → *go to question nine*

       Nope. → *go to question seven*

7. If you had to choose between raisins and peanuts, which would you pick?

       raisins → *go to question eight*

       peanuts → *go to question nine*

8. Which do you drink most of in a day?

   ✗ water, juice, or milk → *go to Scoring Section One*

       soda or anything caffeinated → *go to question ten*

9. Do you frequently leave the lunch or dinner table feeling way too full?

       yes → *go to Scoring Section Three*

       no → *go to question ten*

10. Is there usually food left on your plate at the end of a meal?

       yes → *go to Scoring Section One*

       no → *go to Scoring Section Two*

Healthy Habits

Go-girl traits: You're the healthiest kind of muncher! Totally aware girls like you know that eating right really pays off — you sleep better, look healthier, and get better grades in school!

   Watch out for: Depriving yourself of a certain "bad" food that you're really craving. (You'll just end up munching on more of some other food and still not feel satisfied!) Give in and have a small portion of the food you're craving rather than pigging out on everything else in the kitchen.

Why not try: A fresh fruit smoothie! Here's how:

INGREDIENTS
1 very ripe medium banana, peeled
¾ cup pineapple juice
½ cup low-fat vanilla yogurt
½ cup strawberries (remove the stems!)

UTENSILS
Measuring cup
Blender

WHAT YOU DO:

Pile all the ingredients into the blender and mix till smooth. Makes two servings.

SCORING SECTION TWO:

Middle-of-the-road Muncher

Go-girl traits: You're like most of us — a person who really, really wants to eat healthy, but sometimes you just can't say no to those fries. But as long as you balance the good with the bad, you'll do just fine!

Watch out for: Letting yourself get *too* hungry! When you skip meals (or eat junk food) you get hungry again sooner, which could make you chow down on more Twinkies, 'cause you're dying of hunger! Munch on healthy stuff, like carrot sticks or unsalted pretzels, between meals so you'll stay away from junk instead of getting hungry and losing your willpower.

Why not try: Something yummy but healthy, like banana bread!

INGREDIENTS
2 eggs
1¾ cups sifted flour
2 teaspoons baking powder
¼ teaspoon baking soda
½ teaspoon salt
⅓ cup vegetable shortening
⅔ cup sugar
1 cup mashed bananas (about 3 bananas)

UTENSILS

Beater
Small bowl
Medium bowl
Large bowl
Measuring cups and spoons
Wooden spoon
Bread pan coated with butter, margarine, or a spray like Pam

WHAT YOU DO:

1.   Preheat oven to 350 degrees with a grown-up's help.

2.   Beat eggs well in a small bowl.

3.   In a medium-size bowl, mix together the flour, baking powder, baking soda, and salt with the wooden spoon.

4.   In a large bowl, beat vegetable shortening until it's creamy. Add sugar (a little bit at a time!) and continue beating until the mixture is fluffy.

5.   Add eggs to the goop in the large bowl and beat well.

6.   Add some of the flour mixture to the large bowl and beat well. Then add some mashed banana and beat some more. Continue adding flour, then bananas, then flour, then bananas, until everything's all blended.

7. Pour the mixture into the pan and stick it in the oven for 1 hour and 10 minutes.

8. Flip the pan upside down over a wire rack and let the banana bread cool. Then cut into slices. Yum!

SCORING SECTION THREE:

Junk-food Junkie

Go-girl traits: Hmmm. Let's see. You must *want* to become a healthy eater if you even bothered taking this quiz — and that's the first step toward peeling yourself away from junk food!

Watch out for: You tend to choose quick, convenient foods instead of the ones that are good for you. (How much cash do you spend in vending machines?) If you plan ahead, you can have good-for-you snacks nearby when those hunger pangs start.

Why not try: A good-for-you munchie you can grab on your way out the door, like these celery surprises:

INGREDIENTS
Celery sticks
Peanut butter
Raisins

UTENSILS
Knife
Plastic wrap

WHAT YOU DO:

1. Wash and trim the celery and cut each stick in half.

2. Spread peanut butter inside the celery, from one end to the other.

3. Press raisins into peanut butter.

4. Wrap each one in plastic wrap and stash 'em in the fridge so you can have a quickie health snack handy whenever you're hungry!

Chapter Three

The Supernatural You

Ooh! Spooky weirdness!

OK, so we all crack up at those silly psychic-hot-line infomercials . . . but most of us also flip right to the horoscope page in our favorite mags! Are you a cosmic believer?

WHAT YOUR NAME REVEALS ABOUT YOU

Some people say that the name or nickname you choose to go by can reveal a ton about your innermost personality. Complete this exercise to discover if you're an up-to-your-eyeballs-in-socializing kind of gal or if you are more of a mystery girl.

Directions: Find each letter of your first name

in the chart below. Copy down the number that appears above each letter. Then add the digits together. Once you have your total, add those numbers together until you get a single digit. Then find your forecast next to that number.

Example:

ELIZABETH

5+3+9+8+1+2+5+2+8=43 (total)

[handwritten notes:] 1+1+7+1 = 10
1+1+7+1 = 10 = 1+0 1

Then add the digits of your total together: 4+3=7 (If your total is 10 or more, keep adding the digits together till you get a single number — like, 1+0=1.)

1	2	3	4	5	6	7	8	9
A	B	C	D	E	F	G	H	I
J	K	L	M	N	O	P	Q	R
S	T	U	V	W	X	Y	Z	

Which name should you use? Good question.

- If you go by a nickname when you're with your friends, analyze that name to see what personality traits you display when you're hangin' with them.

- If you go by your first and middle name (like Mary Jo) at school, analyze that name to see what personality traits come across to your teachers.

You can also do your friends' names to see if they have a hidden side you never knew about before!

SCORING

If your name number is . . . 1: You're the Boss.
Is it a coincidence that your name number is one? Since you're a competitive girl who loves to come in first place, we doubt it! You're the first at lots of things: First to raise your hand in class, first to invite the new girl to sit with you at lunch, first to give your speech in class, and first to cut down your competitors. Oops.

One tip: Even real winners lose sometimes and that's okay. Don't view it as failure. Think of it as "sharing the spotlight" and learn to be a good sport.

If your name number is . . . 2: You're Everybody's Best Friend.
One thing you hate is rocking the boat. Like, even if a good friend has disappointed you or flaked on a promise, you probably aren't gonna make a big deal of it. You're also an awesome referee — you can help settle a fight without making anybody feel like a jerk.

One tip: Remember that you deserve to be treated well. If somebody's walkin' all over you,

stand up for yourself — they'll respect you more
for it in the long run.

If your name number is . . . 3: You're the Artist.
Hello, Picasso! Well, maybe your art is talking or
writing instead of painting, but the truth is, you're
one imaginative girl. As a kid, were you always the
one making up the games? And were you just fine
when you got grounded? Having fun all alone is
no struggle for you. Now that you're getting over
your nasty shyness habit, you'll probably find that
you *love* talking to new people.

    One tip: Go ahead and talk to 'em — but make
sure to hush up and listen now and then, too.

**If your name number is . . . 4: You're the Smarty-
pants.**
You just can't help being logical and deep-
thinkin'. Like, when you're at a friend's house for
the day, you probably groove on talking to her
parents at the dinner table. Current events just
sorta click with you, and you love arguing back
and forth with others who know what's going on
in the world. Your friends are really lucky to have
someone like you who's so incredibly loyal.

    One tip: Make an effort to listen to other
people's probs every once in a while. Sometimes
your friends just need a shoulder to cry on instead of solutions to all their troubles.

45

If your name number is . . . 5: You're the Social Butterfly.

Girls with the five name number tend to be superbusy — and they have reeeeally short attention spans! Know how you get bored sitting in certain classes and can't seem to sit still? Energetic girls like you love to be on the go, so in the future you'll probably travel or move to lots of exotic locations. You think stereotypes really stink, and you get inspired when you meet people from different cultures.

One tip: Since so many different interests grab your adventurous spirit, be sure to set clear goals so you don't get sidetracked and forget where you want to go.

If your name number is . . . 6: You're the Girl Next Door.

Do you practically live at the Gap? All your clothes are black, white, or khaki? Girls with the six name number are usually kind of mainstream. That's a great quality to have when it comes to dealing with people 'cause you have a natural knack for solving fights and helping people get along. You should write a book that reveals your secret — how'd you get to be sooo well-liked?

One tip: Although you hate to be an attention hog, you should give some leadership roles a shot.

46

With your smooth attitude, you'd make a great team captain.

If your name number is . . . 7: You're the Mystery Girl.

Lots of alone time — that's what you love. One of your favorite things to do is people-watch. You know, just hang at the mall or the park or out your bedroom window and observe how people walk, talk, or relax. By analyzing other people's mannerisms, you feel like you've connected with someone without risking getting shot down or dissed.

One tip: You have such unique, cool thoughts. We bet lots of people would love to hear them, if you would just open up a little!

If your name number is . . . 8: You're the Dreamer.

You're the one with a heart of gold! It takes a special person to be so giving. You genuinely love helping people. It gives you great happiness to see others live up to their potential — and you'll do almost anything to help them reach their goals. Which makes you really great at motivating people.

One tip: Watch out for being envious of others. If you help a friend accomplish a goal, let her enjoy it and don't try to take the credit. When a truly great idea comes up, it doesn't really matter who gets the credit.

If your name number is . . . 9: You're the Emotional Roller Coaster.

When Valentine's Day rolls around, you're head-to-toe in either pink or black, depending on your current crush status. The thing is, name-number-nine girls like you have a natural romantic flair — you groove on hearing good dating gossip (either your classmates', or celebrities') and you never get tired of giving people friendship and relationship advice. You can get sooo wrapped up in people's lives that it frustrates you when they make stupid choices. You wonder, aren't they listening?

One tip: Keep on being helpful — just don't be overbearing and let people make the final decisions for themselves.

READ YOUR VOWEL!

The first vowel in your name adds an even deeper layer to your name reading. Read into your vowel to personalize your name forecast even more.

Directions: Find the first vowel in your name (*A, E, I, O* or *U*). For example, the name Susan's first vowel is *U*. The letter *Y* counts as a vowel when it sounds like an *E*, as in the name Yvonne.

A: Yours is the Cool Chick vowel — you aren't afraid to stand apart from the crowd.

E: You're so go-with-the-flow, it's amazing. Too bad you're so flaky sometimes!

I: Maybe that *I* stands for "Intensity"! You're totally emotional and get bored easily.

O: Helping people is what you're about. You're so caring!

U: There's always a smile on your face . . . and a decision you're trying to avoid making.

Y: Majorly high goals await you. You just hafta get past your tendency to procrastinate first.

*****

COULD YOU BE PSYCHIC?

Does it sometimes seem like you know what people are gonna say before they say it? Or are you living life minute by minute, never trying to figure out what's around the corner? Find out how much you're into intuition by reading question one, then following the directions next to the answer you choose about which question to jump to next.

1. The last time your teacher sprang a pop quiz on your class, you were somehow prepared.

Spooky but true! → *go to question two*

Not true! → *go to question three*

2. Have you and your friend ever coincidentally bought each other the same exact holiday gift?

    X (yes) → *go to question five*

    (no) → *go to question four*

3. You come back from a weekend of camping and go to your room. Within two seconds you can tell if someone was poking through your stuff while you were away.

        Totally true! → *go to question four*

        No, or it would take me a while. → *go to question six*

4. Does this kind of thing happen to you a lot: You think of a friend you haven't seen in what seems like forever — then you get a call or letter from her the next day?

        Yeah, and it freaks me out! → *go to question five*

        It happened to me once or twice. → *go to question seven*

        Never. → *go to question six*

5. At least once in the past two weeks, you picked up the phone to call your best friend and realized she was trying to call you at the exact same moment!

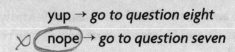

yup → *go to question eight*

✗ (nope) → *go to question seven*

6. If you had a really vivid nightmare about being trapped in the school locker room all night, would you stress out the next day when you had to go in there to change for gym?

sort of → *go to question seven*

not really → *go to question nine*

7. Can you sense when your parents have had a bad day at work even before they walk through the front door?

(yes) → *go to question ten*

✗ (no) → *go to question nine*

8. When your friend tells you who she's secretly crushin' on, can you usually correctly predict whether he'll end up liking her back?

usually → *go to Scoring Section One*

rarely or never → *go to question ten*

9. Have you ever met someone who you immediately thought was very cool — and later found out she was a total meanie?

(yes) → *go to Scoring Section Three*

✗ (no) → *go to question eleven*

10. Do you and your best friend usually know what you each are thinking, even when you're miles apart?

> almost always → *go to Scoring Section One*
>
> sometimes or never → *go to question eleven*

11. If something is wrong with your sister, brother, or other close family member, do you sorta know it deep down inside — even before you find out for sure?

> yeah, frequently → *go to Scoring Section Two*
>
> rarely or never → *go to Scoring Section Three*

SCORING SECTION ONE:

Superpsychic Friend

Whoa. Spooky. Your answers suggest that you are very in tune with your psychic side. People who don't buy the whole cosmic explanation call this ability "intuition" — it's, like, when you know something is going to happen before it actually does. Whatever you wanna call it, it's a skill that helps you choose friends wisely, avoid people in baaaad moods, and maybe even steer clear of some dangerous situations.

SCORING SECTION TWO:

Family Forecaster

OK, so you have some really creepy moments. You know — times when you're sooo close to believing in all this psychic stuff because some eerie mental connection happened between you and your family. Believe it! Your answers reveal that you're skilled at picking up on emotions within your close family circle. And since they're the people you know best, that makes sense, huh? Although this may not be as cool as knowing all your math test answers 24 hours in advance, it can be helpful. Use this sixth sense to judge your parents' moods. That way you can choose the perfect time to ask for that raise in your allowance. . . .

SCORING SECTION THREE:

Cosmically Clueless!

You stick your tongue out at psychic-hot-line commercials. And maybe you even flip right past your horoscope when you're reading a magazine. But since you've gotten *this* far in our quiz, we're pretty sure that you're interested in expanding your psychic skills. With a little concentration, you *can* get better at this stuff. Try paying attention to the body language of family members when they're in good and bad moods. Concentrate on your teacher when she seems totally stressed-out with your class — and be prepared for a massive homework assignment or pop quiz really soon! Sometimes being psychic means you're just using common sense. Once you become more observant, you'll be comfy going along with your gut feelings more often!

*****

WHAT'S YOUR PERSONALITY COLOR?

Believe it or not, everybody's weird mix of personality traits matches up with a particular color of the rainbow. So are you a sunshiny yellow? A fiery red? Discover your color vibe by checking off all the statements that apply to you.

1. ___ People often think I have more money than I really do.

2. ___ People often ask me, "Can't you just sit still?"

3. ___ I'm not the first one to bail on a friend-ship.

4. ___ I tend to end up doing lots of late-night study sessions.

5. ___ I'm good at helping friends resolve fights.

6. ___ Sure, I like my friends, but what I love most is being alone.

7. ✓ It takes me a while to get comfy with people, but once I do, I'm very open.

8. ✓ I'll put up with a problem with one of my friends rather than make a big deal of it.

9. ✓ Whenever I'm around little kids, they always love the games I make up.

10. ___ I'm awesome at science and the arts.

11. ✓ People who don't speak their minds sort of bug me. Like it's my job to figure out what they're thinking?

12. ✓ I have a few different things I am currently collecting.

13. ✓ I'm really interested in hearing what people have to say, but I'm usually too shy to ask questions.

14. ✓ If and when I have a boyfriend, I will probably end up spending less time with my friends.

15. ✓ Whenever I'm assigned a group project, people usually choose me to be the leader.

16. ___ Sometimes my money just seems to disappear! I spend it so fast.

17. ✓ People often think I'm snobby, but I'm really not.

18.____ It isn't enough for me to just join a club — I always want to be the president or v.p.

19.____ No matter what the weather is like, I prefer to be outside.

20.____ I can usually figure out what people are feeling without them saying a word.

21.____ I hug at least one friend every day.

22.____ People seem to cheer up when I walk into the room.

23.____ There isn't much that I'm afraid to do.

24.____ I like to listen and learn more than I like to talk.

25.____ When all of my friends are afraid to go first at something, I'll volunteer.

26.____ Whether it's cooking or cleaning or just helping out, I really enjoy taking care of people.

27.____ I'd prefer to have a small group of really close friends over a large group of pals.

28.____ When I have a crush on a boy, I have a hard time not telling anyone.

29.____ In the mall . . . at school . . . wherever — lots of people seem to ask me for directions.

30.____ I'm really good at building things.

31. ___ I have lots of deep thoughts that I wouldn't even dream of explaining to others. (They'd think I was weird.)

32. ___ I'm not afraid to tell somebody when they make me angry. Sometimes I even yell at my friends.

33. ___ I'll do it if I have to, but I really don't enjoy sharing my stuff.

34. ___ People think I'm secretive.

35. ___ I have a day planner, but I rarely use it.

SCORING:

In the chart below, circle the numbers of all the statements you checked off. Then see which column contains the most circles. Find the letter or letters that appear at the bottom of that column, then read your scoring section below. If you have an equal number circled in two or more columns,

1	2	3	4	5	6	7
8	9	10	11	12	13	14
15	16	17	18	19	20	21
22	23	24	25	26	27	28
29	30	31	32	33	34	35
Y	O	B	R	G	BK	P

read the scoring sections for each of them — you probably display characteristics of both hues.

Y Is for Yellow
Hey, sunshine! A yellow personality like yours fills a room with cheer.

Watch out for: Getting walked on. Because you tend to avoid fights at all costs, people might end up taking advantage of you by not treating you the greatest — they know you won't make a big deal about it.

O Is for Orange
Orange you a busy babe? You live big, which means you're always moving, spending, and having fun.

Watch out for: Being a spotlight hog. Let others be the center of attention sometimes!

B Is for Blue
You're deep and cool — like the big blue ocean — with amazing patience and a thirst for learning.

Watch out for: Coming across a little snobby. People occasionally get freaked out by your quietness.

R Is for Red
Racy, revved-up reds are always in a hurry to lead a team to the finish line.

Watch out for: That red-hot temper — it can get you in trouble!

G Is for Green
On-the-go, outdoorsy green girls love to lend a helping hand.

Watch out for: Being a little selfish with your stuff. Learn to trust others and share.

BK Is for Black
You're surrounded in shadows — not 'cause you're antisocial, but because you're shy and deep in thought.

Watch out for: Getting too much solitude! Connecting with others can really help you grow.

P Is for Pink
Rosy, romantic pinks practically ooze calm! Plus, people feel loved when they're close to you.

Watch out for: Getting lost in your dream-world! Sometimes you have real work to do; fantasies can wait till later — homework can't!

Chapter Four
The Starstruck You

Oh-so-silly celeb stuff!

Milk ads. Magazine covers. Movie posters in your locker. Face it: Stars are just about everywhere you look! How plugged-in are you? Grab a pen and find out!

IS YOUR STYLE SIMILAR TO YOUR STAR'S?

Would you burst into tears if someone stole your hair dryer? Or do you think caring about your looks is pretty superficial? Answer these questions to discover which celebs share your style.

1. *Yawn!* It's Saturday morning — perfect veg-out time! You're planning on some cartoon watching in your pajamas. Then your mom says

she's running to the mall for the day — do you wanna go? (Of course!) You run upstairs and:

a) change into jeans and a T-shirt, grab a baseball cap, and go!

b) jump in the shower, blow-dry your hair, and put on a cute outfit.

c) wash your face, comb your hair, brush your teeth, and change into a casual outfit.

2. How would you describe your hairdo?

a) It's the same one you've had for the last five years, with regular trims.

b) You get a new style every year, maybe in time for back-to-school.

c) It changes a few times a year, depending on your mood.

3. Friends ask you if they can raid your closet when they're looking for:

a) clothes that can be messed up when they're painting or playing sports.

b) something basic, like the perfect sweater or pair of jeans.

c) something special to wear to a party or when they want to look extra-trendy.

4. The idea of playing touch football with your older brother's friends sounds cool because:

a) you'll get to play against people who really know what they're doing!

b) it's different from what you usually do with your friends — and it's cool to hang with your bro every once in a while.

c) there'll be cute boys there! The only bad thing? Playing football.

5. If you got picked to be the major star of a *huge* Hollywood flick, who would you want to walk down the red carpet with you at your movie's premiere?

a) your parents

b) your best friend

c) the cutest boy in school

6. A magazine comes to do a photo shoot at your school. When the editor sees you, she says you'd make a great model — and she wants to take pics of you right now! You:

a) blush and practically run away!

b) let her take a picture or two, then get outta there.

c) let them shoot, like, five rolls.

If you chose MOSTLY A's . . . You're Lovin' That I-live-in-these-jeans Look!

Similar to the celeb styles of: Drew Barrymore, Winona Ryder, Courtney Love, Christina Ricci, Jewel

Your attitude about appearances: If people judge me on my clothes, they aren't my type anyway.

How you rock: You don't fall for appearances. When you're going to approach a potential friend, you aren't scared off by someone's mismatched clothes. In fact, you see that as a sign of originality!

Watch out for: Reverse-stereotyping. Yeah — you're probably used to people making fun of your out-there style. But that doesn't mean you should automatically rule out anybody who's trendy and glam. They could be just as cool as your best friends — in a different kind of packaging.

If you chose MOSTLY B's . . . You're into That Casual-cool Thing.

Similar to the celeb styles of: Jennifer Love Hewitt, Britney Spears, Tia and Tamera Mowry, Gwyneth Paltrow, Katie Holmes

Your attitude about appearances: I wear clothes that match my moods.

How you rock: You can go from comfy to glam

in, like, two seconds. Most styles suit you. You're at ease in supercasual clothes — but for special occasions you'll make the extra effort.

Watch out for: Getting into a style rut! OK, so sometimes you really, really enjoy being comfy — but that doesn't mean you should wear your favorite jeans that you've had forever for the next three years! Even wardrobe basics need updating occasionally.

If you chose MOSTLY C's . . . You Must Live at the Mall!

Similar to the celeb styles of: Brandy, Monica, Danielle Fishel, Jennifer Aniston, Sarah Michelle Gellar

Your attitude about appearances: Looking good helps you feel good.

How you rock: You have confidence when it comes to your appearance. Like, you aren't afraid to be the first one at your school to try out a trend — and that's great.

Watch out for: Thinking less of people who aren't as style-conscious as you. If you only become friends with the most fashionable people, you're being kind of a snob. And you could end up with a circle of friends who look great but annoy you to death!

*****

From 'N Sync to symphonies, there's pretty much music for everybody in the world to enjoy. But some people feel the beat in their hearts, while to others it's just sort of there. What do tunes mean to you? Answer these questions to find out.

1. **Your CD collection is:**

   a) all over the place!

   b) alphabetized or neatly arranged by category — rock, rap, dance, etc.

   c) in a pile or a case, but in no particular order.

2. **When you leave a concert, what are you carrying?**

   a) a T-shirt, two posters, and three buttons

   b) a T-shirt and a Coke

   c) the jacket you came with

3. **When you make a mix tape for your best friend's birthday, what's on it?**

   a) all your favorite songs from the past week, some recorded from the radio

   b) twenty songs that bring back memories from your years of friendship

   c) a few old songs and a few cool, new ones

4. If your friends absolutely hated your favorite band, what would you do?

a) Make them listen to the band if they came on the radio, but you wouldn't force them to endure the whole CD.

b) Listen to your fave group only in private.

c) Tell your buds to really listen again — you're sure they'll love the music if they give it a chance.

5. If you found out that the lead singer of your most favorite band in the world is a drug user, what would your reaction be?

a) You would be really upset and disappointed. It would probably change how much you like them.

b) You wouldn't really care — it's not like you personally know the lead singer or anything!

c) You'd probably avoid going to their concerts, but you'd be OK with listening to their music.

SCORING:

Add up your points, then read your answer section below.

1. a=1, b=3, c=2
2. a=3, b=2, c=1

66

3. a=1, b=3, c=2
4. a=2, b=1, c=3
5. a=3, b=1, c=2

YOUR TOTAL: _____ 7

If you scored 5 to 7 . . . Over That Tune Thing

Music is just background noise to you. Maybe you're more of a visual person — like, are you really into drawing? Watching movies? Taking pictures? Once you find out what creative force drives you, don't be afraid to pursue it.

One tip: If you've spent your whole life never really connecting with music, maybe you just haven't found the right kind yet. Broaden your horizons by listening to different music types, like classical, blues, reggae, jazz, and R & B.

If you scored 8 to 11 . . . You've Got the Beat

Certain songs really get into your soul and stay there forever. But other songs just stop by for a quick visit — like those tunes that you absolutely *love* for a week, then can't stand. You probably aren't the music trendsetter in your group of friends but you do know what you like.

One tip: Ever notice that you like the same bands as all your buds? That's great when concert time rolls around and you can all carpool, but make sure you really like the music that's sucking up all your time (and cash!) and not just buying the CDs to fit in.

If you scored 12 to 15 . . . Mad About Music
Whoa — music really moves you! You're a girl who connects with tunes on practically a spiritual level. Zoning out in your room with your eyes closed, listening to music, is probably one of your favorite things to do. And when you find a band or singer you like, it's almost like making a new friend! That's why you're so bummed when your real-life buds don't share your music tastes — it's practically a personal insult!

One tip: Yes, you probably have great taste when it comes to tunes — but don't become a music snob. Everybody should be free to pick the music that moves them . . . even if you think it stinks!

*****

ARE YOU AN OBSESSED FAN?

Ricky Martin. Prince William. James Van Der Beek. There are sooo many crush-worthy celebs in the world — you can't help drooling over somebody. But has your celeb admiration crossed the line and started to hurt your real-life life? Answer true or false to the following questions to find out if your obsession has turned toxic.

1. When you miss a new episode of your favorite TV show or an appearance of your fave band on TV (and you forget to tape it), you're *really* mad.

(TRUE)   (FALSE)

2. You don't answer the phone while that show is on.

(TRUE)   (FALSE)

3. On your bedroom walls are pics of only one celeb (or his band or show). Nobody else's photos are allowed.

(TRUE)   (FALSE)

4. Your friends automatically call you when they hear news about your celeb crush on *Entertainment Tonight* or *E*.

(TRUE)   (FALSE)

5. You would blow off your best friend's birthday bash in a second if you happened to be invited to a party your fave star was attending the same night.

(TRUE)   (FALSE)

6. You buy any (and every) magazine that mentions your celeb's name on the cover.

(TRUE)   (FALSE)

7. You know your fave celeb's full name, birth date, siblings' names, pets' names, hometown, and lots of other stuff by heart.

(TRUE) (FALSE) ✗

8. In those magazine astrology love-match charts, you have checked to see whether you'd make a great real-life couple.

(TRUE) (FALSE) ✗

SCORING:

Add up the number of times you selected true and read your answer section below.

If you marked six or more statements true . . . 100% Obsessed

You're a total fan! The T-shirts, the books, the posters — you've got 'em all. And as long as you have a fun-filled life outside of your obsession, you're doin' just fine. So here's the big question: Does your love for this celeb hold you back from participating in real life? Like, if you stay inside all weekend because you might win concert tickets on MTV, it's time for a reality check! There are people worth meeting who — unlike your celeb crush — you actually have a chance of getting to know. So get out there and meet some of them!

If you marked three to five statements true . . .
50% Starstruck
Sounds like you have this star-crush thing under control. And even though there are one or two celebs who make you drool, you'd never let those feelings affect your friendships or keep you from participating in real life. Like, it'd be way more fun for you to watch a Backstreet Boys video marathon with your friends than to do it solo. And even though you would *love* to meet your star crush, you have it in perspective: There's a tiny chance it could happen, but for the most part, it's just a really sweet dream!

If you marked two or fewer statements true . . .
0% Celeb Crazy
People who get all gooey over their star crushes totally baffle you. You'd rather spend your time and energy focusing on things that affect you, your friends, and your family. But there's nothing wrong with admiring certain famous people for their talents and accomplishments. Like, if you're a dancer and you love Britney Spears's style, don't be ashamed to say so! Most celebrities have worked really hard to get where they are today — and that's definitely worth respecting!

MAKE YOUR FAN LETTER STAND OUT!

1. Get crafty. Decorate your envelope with stickers, markers, or photos.

2. Get creative. If you're writing to a singer or band, write your letter as new lyrics to their biggest song, or talk (or sing!) into a tape recorder and mail them the tape.

3. Get personal. Instead of writing page after page on how wonderful the star is, write about you — your interests and hobbies, what you and your friends do for fun. You can even send a picture.

4. Get practical. Enclose an envelope with your address already written on it. Also, stick a stamp on it. That way if your celeb gets a sec (a long shot) you might get lucky and get a response!

Chapter Five
The Scholarly You

Class is now in session.

Unlike those you take in school, our pop quizzes are fun. So continue reading and take these quizzes to find out your scholarly style.

ARE YOU A BODY-LANGUAGE MASTER?

Some say you can read people's vibes by studying their actions. So are you sending out "come here" vibes when what you really want to say is "go away"? Discover what signals you're sending out — and find out whether you are reading other people correctly — with these questions.

1. You're sitting through the most booooring slide show in social studies. But thanks to that front-row seat you have, you can't zone out.

How can you make the teacher think you're paying attention while you're actually drifting off into space?

a) Tilt your head and blink a lot.

b) Sit back in your chair with your arms crossed.

c) Lean forward and leave your arms uncrossed.

2. At your BF's family barbecue, the only seat left is next to her really cute older brother. He asks what's up at school and as you answer, you:

a) make eye contact the whole time, not looking away.

b) make eye contact for a few seconds, then look away for a second.

c) keep looking around to make sure everybody notices that he's talking to you.

3. One day at basketball practice, the coach announces she's gonna pick one person to dress up in a dorky mascot outfit for that night's game. How do you act so she's less likely to pick you for this major embarrassment?

a) Stand with your legs apart and your fists unclenched.

b) Put your hands on your hips and frown.

o c) Point your feet toward the door of the gym and look around.

4. You're totally begging your English teacher for an extra night to prepare your essay. After she hears all your excuses (dog ate your homework, virus ate your hard drive . . .), she closes her papers, puts her pen down, and puts her hands flat on the table. What's she gonna say?

    a) You can have an extra night to work.

    b) No extra night!

    c) That you have detention for trying to scam her.

5. Which move *doesn't* show people that you're lying?

    a) touching your face

    b) pulling your ear

    c) clenching your hands

SCORING:

Add up your total below, then read your answer section.

        1. a=5, b=0, c=10

        2. a=5, b=10, c=0

        3. a=0, b=5, c=10

4. a=10, b=0, c=5
5. a=0, b=0, c=10
YOUR TOTAL: _15_

If you scored 0 to 10 . . . You've Got All the Wrong Moves.

Have you ever noticed that you always get picked for the stinky school projects? That when you expect to get yelled at by a teacher, she's really about to praise your awesome work? Well, it's because your body-lingo skills need some tweaking. Right now you tend to send out vibes that mean the exact opposite of what you're trying to say!

Our suggestion: Go back to the quiz above, and check out the scoring section for the highest-scoring answers — they're the good-body-lingo ones. Then use those moves from now on to convey what you want!

If you scored 15 to 30 . . . You Know a Few Tricks.

It's great that you aren't afraid to use your body to send out messages; now you just have to work on saying the right things! See, your moves are a little on the unnatural side — like, you know you should make eye contact with people, but you maybe end up in a staring match instead of just being casual about it!

Remember this rule: When it feels forced, chill out and act natural. You'll get the hang of it soon!

If you scored 35 to 50 . . . You're Fluent in Body Lingo!

You're able to speak very loudly with even the littlest moves — and that's a powerful skill to have. It means you can subtly let a boy know you aren't into him without having to come out and say it. And maybe you can wordlessly let Coach know you'd really rather *not* dress up in that toad costume in front of the whole school.

One rule for you: Even though you're great at body language, don't rely on it when you need to get a clear message across. (The person you're talking to might not pick up on your clues.) When what you're saying *really* matters, say it.

*****

WHAT'S YOUR STUDY STYLE?

Taking a hard look at your studying habits is a good way to predict your success in school. Are you trying too hard — or maybe not hard enough? Find out by answering these questions, then read on for cool school tips from real girls like you.

1. What's your first thought when the teacher assigns a group project?

X a) Cool! Now I can hang with my friends — it'll make studying much more fun.

b) How can I hook up with the class brain? That'll pretty much guarantee me an A.

c) Oh, man — that's gonna bring my grade down.

2. What's your favorite study spot like?

a) Someplace quiet where nobody will interrupt me — like my bedroom. I need total peace and quiet to really focus and do my best.

b) The library — that way I can be around friends, yet still concentrate.

c) Near the TV or radio — the noise helps time pass more quickly.

3. Which of the following items are in your school bag? (Check all that apply.)

- ✓ two pens ✓
- ✓ two pencils ✓
- highlighter ✓
- ✓ day planner ✓
- ✓ calculator ✓

4. Highlighters: Love 'em or hate 'em?

a) Love — without them I'd fail! ✓

b) Hate — they're annoying!

5. When you get to class, what's the first thing you do?

a) Say hi to your friends, then sit down and get ready before the bell rings.

b) Go straight to your desk and get your stuff out — no chitchat for you.

c) Grab your friend to chat — and most of the time you keep talking till the teacher asks you to stop.

SCORING:

Add up your points, then read your answer section below.

1. a=2, b=1, c=3   2

2. a=3, b=2, c=1   3

3. Add three points for each item you checked.   2

4. a=3, b=1   2

5. a=2, b=3, c=1

YOUR TOTAL: _28_

If you scored 4 to 11 . . . Slackin'!
Your study style: Mellow and laid-back, you don't like to freak about schoolwork. While you may not be stressing now about finishing that home-

79

work, it'll catch up with you eventually — like on report-card day!

Smart moves to try: A few small steps can move you closer to Good Student-ville — keeping a day planner, making the effort to write your notes neatly, highlighting key words, that kind of stuff. Once your grades show a little improvement, you might actually enjoy studying and learning!

If you scored 12 to 19 . . . Shining!
Your study style: OK — so you're realistic when it comes to studying. You know that if you deprive yourself of all social time, you might go nuts! And by finding a way to fit both friends *and* homework into your day, you can stay sane and be a good student, too.

Smart moves to try: When there's an assignment that carries lots of weight, put in the extra effort — even if it brings your daily fun down a notch. Like, if your term paper counts for half your grade, step away from the phone . . . and the e-mail . . . and the group study sessions, because it's time to focus! Otherwise, you're doing fine.

If you scored 20 to 27 . . . Stressin'!
Your study style: Hello, overachiever! You're a serious student who's loved big-time by teachers. Getting the highest grade in class rocks your

world, and you love it when the teacher asks you to read your papers aloud in class.

Smart moves to try: You should be proud of yourself — learning is really important, and you realize that. But don't you feel a little cheated sometimes? Like when everyone else is out at the mall on a Friday afternoon and you're stuck at home with your flash cards? The key to being happy is balance! By taking a few minutes before class to chat with friends, and generally making room for some social life, you'll feel more energized — and still have time left to get that A+!⚡

STUDY SECRETS FROM REAL GIRLS

"If I have to study for a long time, I take a five-minute break every hour and call my friends. It's like a little reward." — Jacki, 12, California

"I would *die* without my date book! When I have something major due for school, I write a countdown on my calendar so I end up freaking out about it every day. That gets me moving." — Deidre, 13, Pennsylvania

"When we're studying a subject that's really boring, I'll go home and look it up on the Web. I can usually find cool sites that help me understand the subject a little better (and without falling asleep!)." — Alexis, 11, Nevada

> "My best friends and I always study together. That way we aren't afraid to ask each other stupid questions that we were too embarrassed to ask in front of the whole class." — Tamara, 10, Ohio

*****

ARE YOU RIGHT-BRAINED OR LEFT-BRAINED?

Scientists say that your creativity and logic skills are affected by a weird thing: which half of your brain is more dominant. So are you an ultra-organized lefty or an amazingly artistic righty? Check off all the statements that sound like you and find out if you are right- or left-brained dominant. Then discover how you can expand the opposite side of your brain to become more well-rounded.

✓ 1. My notebooks are really neat and tidy.

✓ 2. Most of the time my room is a total disaster area.

✓ 3. If I needed ten friends' addresses, I would just have to look in my address book — they'd all be in there alphabetically.

___ 4. I'm pretty artistic.

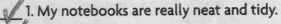

_____ 5. I make my bed almost every morning.

√ 6. When I'm browsing at the bookstore, I'll buy a book if it has a cool or interesting cover even if I really don't know what it's about.

_____ 7. Without me, my friends wouldn't know what to do on the weekends.

√ 8. When I'm in the mood to listen to music, I'll look through my CD collection and choose something just right instead of turning on the radio.

√ 9. I exercise at a certain time or place every day or week.

√ 10. I get distracted really easily.

√ 11. I have to outline a paper before I can actually start writing.

√ 12. I think making last-minute plans is exciting and fun.

√ 13. I'm awesome at memorizing things.

√ 14. If I have a major fight with my family or a friend, I'll do something afterward that makes me feel better, like going for a long walk or eating an ice-cream cone.

50 6F

Add up how many even- and odd-numbered statements you checked. Then read your answer section below.

If you picked mostly odds you are: Left-brainy

Cool qualities:

- You're always so on time!
- You're great at analyzing, memorizing, and making decisions based on what you think.
- Planning comes easily to you — you're the one who makes sure everybody knows when and where you're meeting.
- You're totally level-headed.

Watch out for:

- Talking too much! You're always trying to explain yourself.
- Getting too obsessed with schedules and being organized.

Explore your right-brainy side by:

- Writing in a journal as soon as you wake up — before your logical mind kicks in.
- Setting aside time to be creative — like an hour to play with waterpaints or sketch.
- Using those awesome memorization skills to remember a bunch of funny jokes.

If you picked mostly evens you are: Right-brainy

Cool qualities:

- You're very artistic and creative.
- Last-minute plans don't make you anxious.
- You're so in touch with your feelings.
- You can see the big picture instead of getting all caught up with the little details.

Watch out for:

- Going with your gut feelings when what you really need to do is use your brain — sometimes decisions shouldn't be made based on emotions alone.
- Being disorganized — make an effort to get it together!

Explore your left-brainy side by:

- Not just coming up with an idea about what to do on Saturday night — next time be the one who organizes the whole plan!
- Putting your creativity to work at school! Maybe giving a speech in front of your class wouldn't be so scary if you presented it as a scene from a play or by pretending to be a newscaster.
- Making a list of pros and cons before making important decisions to be sure you're making the right choice.

*****

DO YOU HAVE A HIDDEN ARTISTIC SIDE?

Are you the next great painter? Future Oscar-winning actress? A Grammy-winner-to-be? Reveal your hidden talents with these simple questions.

Section One

☑ You're great at English, history, or foreign languages.

___ You prefer essay tests over true/false or multiple choice tests.

☑ When you're in a fight with your best friend, you'd rather write her a note or e-mail instead of confronting her in person.

☑ When you read a book, you often picture the story like a movie in your head.

☑ You really like hanging out by yourself.

Section Two

___ You have a huge music collection that's your prized possession.

☑ You always sing — in the shower, in the car, everywhere.

☑ You've always wanted to learn to play a certain musical instrument.

___ You love being the center of attention.

___ When a friend is in a bad mood, you know the perfect song to cheer her up.

Section Three

☑ You aren't klutzy at all. ✓

☑ You're always trying new sports or new dance moves.

☑ You're very flexible.

☑ You don't get too freaked-out by crowds. ✓

☑ You exercise at least three times a week, ✓ for a half hour or more each time.

Section Four

☑ When you get a roll of film developed, the photos you've shot are always great. ✓

☑ Your wardrobe is a mix of many colors and prints. ✓

☑ You always remember a face, but sometimes you forget the person's name.

☑ In class, you tend to doodle a lot. And some of your doodles are pretty cool-looking.

☑ People say you have really funky or cool handwriting.

SCORING:

Find the section in which you checked the most statements, then read that answer section below to find out where your talents lie.

Answer Section One: The Writer

Your skills: Putting feelings and thoughts down on paper in an interesting, creative way.

How you can get artsy: Write short stories or poetry. Create your own Web site. Be the organizer of your school newspaper's poetry corner.

Answer Section Two: The Music Maker

Your skills: Understanding music — like, what mood it conjures up and how it makes listeners feel.

How you can get artsy: Learn to play an instrument (or two), make mix tapes, sing, or be the DJ at your friends' parties.

Answer Section Three: The Mover

Your skills: You are able to pick up new dance moves and sports really quickly and can master them much faster than the average person.

How you can get artsy: Take dance classes, check out your school's drama department, and learn tricks on your bike, blades, or skateboard.

Answer Section Four: The Traditional Artist

Your skills: Creating cool and striking visual images by knowing what shapes, colors, and textures go great together.

How you can get artsy: Design clothes, take photos, learn calligraphy, paint, or sketch.

Chapter Six
The Friendly You

All about the girls in your <u>life</u>!

The friends you choose — and how you treat them — reveals a lot about what's important to you and what makes you tick. What's *your* friendship factor?

Do you have the receiver practically glued to your ear? Or do you kind of bum out when you hear that ringer ringin'? To find out if the phone is your BFF or your most evil enemy, answer these questions.

1. You're cuddled up all cozy on the couch, about to take a trip to Nap Land when (of

course!) the phone rings. What's your plan of action?

a) Let the answering machine get it.

✗ (b) You're so there before it even has a chance to ring twice.

c) Drag yourself off the couch and get to the phone before the machine gets it.

2. *Crash!* A major storm wipes out all the phone lines in your town — and they won't be fixed for three days! How much will your life be changed?

a) Majorly! You don't know what to do with the hour or two of spare time you have on your hands. You miss the friendly buzz of the dial tone.

b) Slightly, but maybe now you'll be motivated to actually walk over to your friends' houses and chat in person.

✗ (c) Not much. In fact, it'll be cool not to hear the phone ringing all the time!

3. A friend of your mom's needs a baby-sitter at the last minute — the pay is great and the kids are two little angels! All you have to do is call and tell her about your experience. What do you do?

✗ (a) Call ASAP and tell her all about your baby-sitting success stories!

90

b) Forget it — if she really wanted your services, she'd call you.

c) Call and wait for her to ask you questions, kind of like an interview.

4. Grandma calls to wish you a happy b-day and then she asks you about a zillion questions so she can catch up with everything that's going on in your life. How does your side of the convo go?

a) You answer her questions in a few quick words.

b) You answer her questions, then ask a few back to be polite.

c) You fill her in on all the latest news — from crushes to classes to cool shows you saw on TV.

5. You and your best friend discover you both have a crush on the same boy — and it turns into a massive fight. After a few days of not talking to her, you realize that *no* boy is worth losing your best friend over, so you:

a) call her and have a major heart-to-heart over the phone.

b) track her down first thing at school the next day so you can talk in person.

c) call her and see if you can stop by 'cause

91

you have something important to talk about.

6. Check off all the following statements that sound like you.

_✓_ I have my own phone line.

___ I always prank-call the boy I like, just to hear him say, "Hello?"

_✓_ Usually I do most of the talking when I'm on the phone with a friend.

_✓_ I would go totally nuts if I had to talk on a phone with a cord.

_✓_ I always answer call waiting, even when I'm in the middle of a really important conversation.

___ I can do lots of things while I'm talking on the phone: wash the dishes, do homework, whatever.

7. Check off all of the following statements that sound like you.

_✓_ I doodle or watch TV while I talk on the phone.

___ When I'm on the phone with a really chatty friend and I want to get off, I tell her a little white lie, like "My mom needs the phone."

✓ I have a hard time understanding how my friends can talk on the phone for hours.

___ I'll take the phone off the hook when I'm not in the mood to chat.

___ Cellular phones are *so* annoying!

SCORING:

Add up your points and read your answer section below.

1. a=5, b=15, c=10
2. a=15, b=10, c=5
3. a=15, b=5, c=10
4. a=5, b=10, c=15
5. a=15, b=5, c=10
6. Add 15 for each statement you checked.
7. Add 15 for each statement you *left blank*.

YOUR TOTAL: ____

If you scored 25 to 100 . . . Hello? Hello? Is Anyone There?

There are two things your score could mean. Either you're so busy with after-school activities and sports that you simply don't have the time to talk on the phone (which is cool). Or maybe you're kind of freaked-out or shy about communicating with people. If that's the case, you need to work on your phone skills, 'cause the way you chat probably makes people feel like they're boring you! Good phone skills can get you really far. They can help you score that after-school job . . . a great interview for the school paper . . . maybe even an extra hour on your curfew! So don't be in such a rush to end your phone chats. Relax, talk, and listen.

If you scored 105 to 170 . . . I Hear What You're Saying!

You see the phone as a convenient thing — definitely not a necessity for keeping in touch with people you see every day. You can use the phone to set up in-person hang-out sessions with the people you love — not as a replacement for face-to-face interaction. While lots of people spend time indoors talking, you're outside livin' life to its fullest! However, you also know that the phone can help you stay tight with people who aren't within hugging distance. Keep doing what you're doing — you're totally effective on the phone!

If you scored 175 to 240 . . . Please Hang Up and Try Again!

Looks like all circuits are busy in your house — all the time! Unless you have your own line (and even if you do), your parents probably bug you about the hours (and hours, and hours) you spend with that receiver attached to your ear. And while it's awesome that you're so social and friendly, some of your answers indicate that you're a major spotlight-hogger on the phone. Like, is most of the chat time spent discussing *your* loves and hates and everything in between? If this sounds so familiar it's scary, make an effort to listen sometimes. Your friends deserve their fair share of attention, too.

FIVE COOL ANSWERING MACHINE RECORDINGS

Forget that boring "Please leave a message at the beep" stuff! Record one of these funky messages on your machine instead. . . .

- "Hello? HELLO? I can't hear you — is something wrong with your phone? [long pause] Just kiddin'. Leave me a message . . ."
- "Welcome to Burger King! May I take your order? No? Okay, well, leave a message at the beep instead."
- "Hi! [Your name]'s answering machine is broken. This is her refrigerator. Please speak very slowly and I'll stick your message to myself with one of these magnets."

- "The number you have reached, [your number], has been changed. The new number is [your number again]. Please make a note of it. Ha-ha . . . no, just leave me a message!"

*****

WILL YOU BE FRIENDS FOREVER? (A TWO-PERSON QUIZ!)

You love each other like sisters — but will your friendship last through thick and thin? What seem like little problems now could turn into biggies later on. Take this quiz to find out if you and your BF have what it takes to be BFF.

Read each statement below and grade it on a separate sheet of paper — give it a three if it's very true for you, a two if it's sometimes true, and a one if it's false. Then have your best friend read and grade the statements on a separate piece of paper, too. Read the scoring section to see how long-lasting your friendship is likely to be.

1. My best friend and I have the exact same taste in boys.

2. It takes me a while to return the clothes I borrow from her.

3. I have lied to her.

4. She hardly ever calls when she says she will.

5. Sometimes I feel like she takes her stinky moods out on me.

6. She let one of my big secrets slip out.

7. I have a lot of interests that she knows nothing about.

8. Sometimes I feel like she's trying to make me feel bad.

9. If I have a totally busy week, she gets mad at me for not having enough time for her.

10. She talks about her problems all the time and rarely asks how I'm doing.

11. If we were both trying for the same part in the school play and she got it, I'd be resentful and not totally happy for her.

12. She has bailed on plans with me when something better has come up.

13. She gets really mad when I have to cancel plans with her.

14. I haven't been having a lot of fun with her lately, but if I bailed on her, she would have no friends.

15. She only comes around or calls when her other friends bail on her.

SCORING:

Each of you adds up your ones, twos, and threes on your own sheet of paper. Then add your totals together and read your answer section below.

If you scored 30 to 50 . . . Stuck Like Glue
The bonus: Congrats! Your friendship is mature and respectful. Even during the tough times, you stick together and help each other.

    Watch out for: Since you guys get along so awesomely, the only trap you might fall into is getting *too* comfortable! Like, if you think you know everything there is to know about each other, you're wrong — each of you is gonna keep growing and changing. So if you want to stay as close as you are right now, make time for regular heart-to-hearts where you can really share what you both are thinking and feeling.

If you scored 51 to 70 . . . Stick Around
The bonus: Between the two of you, you have most of the equipment needed to be friends forever. Now you just have to make sure you're both making equally as strong an effort to stay buds.

    Watch out for: Letting one person do all the talking — that's sooo not fair! If one of you is very chatty and the other is sort of quiet, you still should make talk time equal. You both need to be open with each other. It'll bring the two of you closer.

If you scored 71 to 90 . . . Sticky Friendship Situation

The bonus: Your friendship is really exciting. Some days it's up, some days it's down — you never know whether you're gonna want to hug or strangle each other! But even though you might fight a lot, since you're taking this quiz together, it looks like you're both willing to work hard to turn this friendship into gold.

Watch out for: Betraying each other's trust during one of the rough patches — ouch! The truth is, you guys have a few areas of your friendship that need some work. You should promise each other that even during your worst fights, you won't badmouth and trash-talk each other. You'll wait till you both cool off, then talk about it together. It's a great start that'll help you build trust.

"My best friend is reliable, loyal, and most of all, funny. She knows the perfect thing to say when I'm really bummed out." — Samantha, 11, New Jersey

"1. She's the only one who I trust with my secrets; 2. She treats me like one of her sisters, which is really cool since I'm an only child; 3. She supports me when I'm really afraid of doing something, like trying out for the soccer team." — Jen, 10, Maryland

"I have so much fun with my best friend — we never stop laughing. And she's also really honest and friendly. I'm not as shy since I started hanging out with her." — Beth, 12, California

*****

ARE YOU TOO CLIQUEY?

Sure, everybody wants to be liked — but do you choose your friends based on what other people think of them and whether they're cool? Are you friends with people you don't really like just because other people think you should be? Or are you so anticliquey that you snub people who might make really good friends just because they are in a particular group? Check off all the statements that sound like you.

X ✓ 1. I sometimes go along with what my friends are doing, just so I don't seem like a party pooper even when I don't really want to do it.

✓ 2. If all your friends are teasing a girl you know is really sweet, you stick up for her.

___ 3. If you can't go to the mall on Saturday with your friends because you have soccer practice, they'll be mad at you.

___ 4. You find out that a sweet (but shy) boy has a crush on you. All your friends laugh and say what a dork he is. You hang out with him anyway.

___ 5. You would pass up a day at the beach with your family so you could hang out with your friends.

X ✓ 6. Your mom says she'd be so disappointed if you ever went to a party that wasn't supervised by adults. One of your friends knows about a party an older girl is throwing but her parents are away and won't be there. All your friends are going. You still say no.

X ___✓___ 7. Your friends are all gonna try out for the cheerleading squad. Even though you've never held a pom-pom in your life, you tag along and try out, too, because otherwise you'd feel left out.

X ___✓___ 8. You have made more than three new friends this year.

   ___✓___ 9. Your friend is mad at a girl you know — and she asks you to join her in giving this girl the silent treatment. You, of course, help her out even though you don't have anything against this girl personally.

X ___✓___ 10. You don't hang out with the same exact group of friends every weekend.

SCORING:

Give yourself ten points for every even-numbered statement you checked. Now subtract from your total five points for every odd-numbered statement you checked to get your final score.

If you scored 0 to 30 . . . Totally Cliqued
Danger! You're a group groupie — and that means the friends you spend most of your time with may not be true friends at all. See, cliques are weird because they cause you to pretend to like people who haven't earned your trust or respect and who

you don't really consider true friends. And when you create friendships for fake reasons (like based on the way people dress, where they live, or what team they're on), they crumble easily. Unless you crush this cliquey thinking, you might find yourself alone really soon or doing things you really don't want to do.

What to do: Admit it: You've met nice people who you didn't become friends with 'cause they weren't in your clique. Promise yourself that you'll try never to do that again.

If you scored 35 to 50 . . . Sick of Cliques

It's cool chicks like you who really rule the school. And even though you might not *feel* like the most popular girl, you have something that social butterflies don't have: Real friends who love you for all the right reasons. You pride yourself on your individuality — and it's probably one of the things your friends really dig about you, too. Not only do they respect you, but *you* respect you — and that's a great feeling.

What to do: Keep it up! Your close circle of buds will probably stick with you for a long time. One thing to watch out for: Do you avoid people in certain cliques because you assume they're snobs? Or maybe you don't talk to them because you're (a little) intimidated? Get over it. A cool girl like you has no need for labels. You should judge all people for yourself, not based on the opinions of others.

*****

ARE YOU A NOTE JUNKIE?

Do you spill your deepest, darkest secrets to your pals in the notes you write during class? Or are notes just a quick way for you to say hey? Discover what's right (and what might be wrong) with your in-class communication style by answering these questions.

1. You've received detention from being busted by your teacher for passing notes.

 X

2. You know at least ten different ways to fold your notes.

X

3. You have all your notes stashed away somewhere safe — even the ones from a couple years ago.

4. If you saw a note on your sister's dresser, you would read it.

X

5. You've gotten in *serious* trouble when someone read something incriminating in one of your notes.

(TRUE) (FALSE) X

6. You've done that *Felicity* thing — you know, where you record your notes to friends on tapes.

(TRUE) (FALSE) X

7. You exchange two or more notes with each friend per day.

(TRUE) (FALSE) X

8. You and your friends use a code language and code names in your notes.

X (TRUE) (FALSE) X

9. Over the summer, you write tons of letters to your friends when you're at camp or on a vacation (or if *they're* at camp or away).

(TRUE) (FALSE) X

10. You have a special notebook you use for writing notes.

(TRUE) (FALSE) X

Add up the number of times you answered true, then read your section below.

If you marked one to three trues . . . You're an In-person Person.

Your daily note quota: One or maybe two, if you're really bored in study hall.

What kinds of topics you cover: What you're going through that day — if you're tired, bored, annoyed, whatever. But mostly you only use notes to tell friends that you need to talk to them — you'd rather not get into really personal stuff on paper. (You'd freak out if someone else read it!)

Cool suggestions for cooler notes: Since you're such a great talker, try recording rambling letters on a tape recorder when you can't hang with your friends in person.

If you marked four to seven trues . . . You're a Comfy Chatterer.

Your daily note quota: Usually around three or four. But if there's something major going on, you may end up writing five or more.

What kinds of topics you cover: Boys (!), problems that you need your friend's help with.

Cool suggestions for cooler notes: Share a journal with your best friend. Like, you take it home one night to write in it, then give it to her the next day in school. That night she takes it home, writes back, and returns it to you the next day. It'll help keep your notes organized — and it'll turn into a cool journal of your friendship! You'll also be less likely to miss something important in class while writing or reading a note — and this way you can't get caught for passing them, either.

If you marked eight to ten trues . . . You're a Note Nut.

Your daily note quota: At least five, sometimes more — *way* more!

What kinds of topics you cover: How your friend annoyed you, how this class is sooo boring, what boy you're crushin' on, a fight you had with your parents, that weird dream you had last night . . . anything and everything goes!

Cool suggestions for cooler notes: Sometimes shorter is better! Although we *love* the fact that you're so great at putting your feelings down on paper, remember this: You're giving that paper away to someone else and you never know when your friend's mom or big brother will end up reading all about your private business! Besides, by spending that much time writing and reading notes, you're surely missing some major stuff in class — and this is bound to affect your grades in the long run. Our tip: Start paying more attention to your teacher and save the personal stuff for your journal or private conversations with friends.

*****

ARE YOU A GOOD LISTENER?

Do friends always come to you for help with their biggest, baddest probs? Or do they not even bother telling you when they're going through a tough time because they know it'll be in one ear, out the other? Answer these questions and find out if you're a good listener, then read on for tips on how to help a friend in need.

1. You offer your friends and classmates advice when:

 a) they ask (which is often).

 b) you have a personal story you want to share that has to do with what they're going through.

 c) you think they might get into trouble if you don't say something.

2. Do you ask lots of questions when you don't understand what your friend is telling you about what she's going through?

 a) Yes — I think asking her questions helps her figure her probs out for herself.

b) A few here and there — I usually just wait till there are quiet (awkward!) spots in the convo.

c) No way — I'm just there to listen, and a good listener doesn't interrupt.

3. Are you good at keeping secrets — even really, really juicy ones?

a) Yes. I might tell my best friend, but that's it — and I always swear her to secrecy.

b) Pretty much — but I have to admit that occasionally I've let secrets slip out.

c) I always, always keep them locked up tight!

4. How's your memory?

a) Pretty stinky sometimes!

b) Awesome — I remember most conversations practically word for word.

c) Good with some things, bad with others.

5. One day you notice that a close friend looks majorly bummed. When you ask her what's up, she says that she just found out that her parents are getting divorced. What do you say?

a) "I'm so sorry." But you don't dig any further in case she doesn't want to talk about such a majorly personal thing.

b) "Are you OK? Do you want to talk about it?"

X c) "It'll be weird for a while, but you'll be fine — lots of parents get divorced." That way she doesn't feel alone.

6. Has anybody ever told you that you interrupted them when they were talking?

X a) yes

b) no

7. Do you get annoyed when people make a huge deal out of their problems?

X a) Kind of — they end up sounding sort of whiny!

b) Sometimes, like when people go on and on for*ever*! But mostly I understand it 'cause people need to vent.

c) Not really. If they go overboard or I'm not really in the mood to listen, I'll just bail on the conversation.

SCORING:

Add up your points below, then read your answer section to rate your listening skills.

1. a=3, b=1, c=2
2. a=3, b=2, c=1

3. a=2, b=1, c=3

4. a=1, b=3, c=2

5. a=2, b=3, c=1

6. a=1, b=3

7. a=1, b=3, c=2

YOUR TOTAL: _15_

If you scored 7 to 10 . . . "I Know How You Feel!"
You like to listen — to yourself, that is! And although being a good talker is way important, sometimes your friends are gonna need you to open up your ears to them . . . without jumping in with your own stories and dilemmas! Truth is, that kind of "listening" will make your friends feel like you don't care (which is *so* not true!). Check out the next page for five easy steps that'll help you become a better listener.

If you scored 11 to 16 . . . "My Ears Are Sorta Open."
Your listening skills are at their best when you're talking to someone who's really open about their problems. Where you get stuck, though, is when somebody's so bummed that they don't know how to tell you what's wrong. Don't be afraid to ask — especially when you're talking to good friends. Read the tips below and learn how to listen without feeling like you're digging for gossip.

If you scored 17 to 21 . . . "I Hear What You're Sayin'."

Wow! Your buds are so lucky to have such a good listener as their friend. You know how to ask the right questions and when to keep quiet, and you're probably really proud of the help you give your friends. The only problem facing good listeners like you is this: Do you ever feel like everybody pours their heart out to you, but no one ever asks how *you're* feeling in return? Your friends probably just think that you're so good at solving problems that you don't have any of your own! Open up and give them the chance to listen and help *you* for a change — they're your friends so we're sure they'll wanna.

FIVE STEPS TO HELP A BUMMED-OUT BUD

1. Ask questions. How will you know what's on someone's mind unless you ask? A lot of times people don't know how to start talking about stuff, so you can help out with questions. Don't ask ones they can answer with just a yes or no — we're talkin' questions that make them think and get to the botttom of things.

2. Don't interrupt. Unless your friend is saying the same thing over and over, or you're really confused about something she said, let her talk.

3. Wait to be asked for help. Sometimes people just need to vent — they don't really want you to solve their problems for them. So listen and ask questions — but keep your opinions to yourself unless she seems to want them.

4. Let her find her own answer. Everybody hates bossy people. Your best advice-givin' bet? Help your friend find the answer for herself. For example, if the dilemma is about getting more allowance, ask questions like, "How did you get your parents to raise it last year? Why do you think they're saying no now?" To help her figure out herself what she can do.

5. Remember to follow up. After your friend has opened up to you, the next time you talk to her, ask her how she is and how everything is working out. It lets her know you really care.

*****

WHAT'S YOUR E-MAIL STYLE?

We all agree that zapping off quick e-mails is a *way* convenient way to keep in touch with people. Most of us write ten times more e-mails than actual letters — but not everyone relies on this electronic form of communication! Would you burst into tears if your parents took your computer away — or maybe not even notice? Answer the questions below and follow instructions about what question to go to next to find out your e-mail style.

1. Do you often use a smiley face symbol :—) instead of saying how funny something is, how happy you are, or that you're joking around?

       yes → *go to question two*

   x (no) → *go to question three*

2. Do you like to use at least three exclamation points when you announce big news?

       yes → *go to question five*

       no → *go to question four*

3. Are your e-mails often superlong — like, pages and pages?

       yes → *go to question six*

   x (no) → *go to question four*

4. Do you usually write in choppy phrases instead of long sentences?

       yes → *go to question seven*

   x (no) → *go to question six*

5. Do you skip the salutation (like, "Dear Jen . . .") and just dive right into your message, as if you're talking face-to-face?

yes → *go to question eight*

no → *go to question seven*

6. Do you have a particular e-pal who you exchange messages with several times a week?

yes → *go to question nine*

X no → *go to question ten*

7. Do you forward all the chain e-mails that people send you to your other pals?

yes → *go to question eight*

no → *go to question ten*

8. You keep most of your old e-mails from friends filed away in mailboxes.

yes → *go to Scoring Section Two*

no → *go to question eleven*

9. Do you feel like you might die if your e-mail was out of order for a week?

yes → *go to question twelve*

no → *go to question ten*

10. Today you get an e-mail from your second cousin who you really like but only get to see once a year. Do you write back within the day?

X yes → *go to Scoring Section Two*

no → *go to question eleven*

11. You almost always write something funny in the subject line so your friends will crack up the minute they see your e-mail pop up.

> yes → *go to Scoring Section One*
>
> no → *go to Scoring Section Two*

12. You put so much work into the e-mails you send to friends that you like to keep a copy of all the long ones you send out.

> yes → *go to Scoring Section Three*
>
> no → *go to Scoring Section Two*

SCORING SECTION ONE:

Queen of the "Forward" Function

You see e-mail as a big joke factory, and that's cool. You like to forward funny messages to your friends that you know will brighten up their day. You're probably also great at tracking down funny pictures and comics to e-mail your friends.

Watch out for: Forwarding every single piece of junk e-mail you receive! If you keep sending all your friends chain mail, they just might stop looking forward to getting e-mails from you.

SCORING SECTION TWO:

So Over Snail Mail

You treat e-mail just like people used to use regular mail — as a way to keep in touch with faraway friends and family. It's a supersimple way to stay tight with people you love without all the hassle of stamps and envelopes.

Watch out for: Giving up the snail mail thing altogether. Face it: Mailing somebody the perfect birthday card is cool 'cause they can keep it in their scrapbook forever. For some reason an e-postcard just doesn't seem quite as special!

SCORING SECTION THREE:

Serious about E-mail

To you, e-mail is just like talking to somebody in person. You put lots of care into your messages, and it's likely that you have tons o' pen pals who keep your e-mailbox overflowing with love.

Watch out for: Letting e-friendships take priority over real ones. And no matter how cool or trustworthy somebody you meet on the Internet seems to be, never give them your real name, address, or phone number.

EMOTICONS

When you're writing a quickie e-mail, there often isn't time to go into detail about how or what you're feeling. You can use these little icons to convey your emotions. (That's why they're called emoticons!)

:-(	Frowning face conveys being sad or upset
:-)	Regular smiley face — means you're happy
=:-O	Face with open mouth conveys surprise
8-)	Smiley face with glasses means you're happy
:-x	Means you're sending kisses
:-$	Smiley face with braces
>:-P	Face with tongue sticking out expresses being grossed-out

And some extra treats:

(^.—-.^)	Kitten
@——-^—-^—	Rose with thorns

*****

WHAT KIND OF FRIEND ARE YOU?

People are like snowflakes — every one is different. But there *are* certain types of people who share common characteristics. And when it comes to being a friend, most of us end up being a certain type of friend, too. So are you the teacher, the talker, the tickle-your-funny-bone girl? Check off all the statements below that sound like you to find out what kind of bud you usually are.

X ✓ 1. I can always get my friends to laugh.

   2. My friends have spent sooo many hours helping me through my problems.

✓ 3. I'm really good at getting friends to make up after a big fight.

✓ 4. I like it when friends challenge me to do stuff that intimidates me, like running for student government, trying out for a sports team, or auditioning for the school play.

✓ 5. Friends always come to me when they're upset; they say I make them feel better.

✓ 6. In, like, 90 percent of my conversations with friends, boys are the main topic.

   7. I sometimes cancel plans at the last minute because I just don't feel like going out.

✓ 8. When a friend gets mad at me for no reason, I don't worry — I know it'll be OK.

✓ 9. If I'm about to do something that my friends think is strange, I'd totally want them to talk to me about it.

✓ 10. I always go to my friends' games to cheer them on.

✓ 11. People say I tell the greatest jokes.

___ 12. Everybody knows I'm really sensitive — like, I always cry at sad movies.

✗ ✓ 13. I try not to take sides when my friends are fighting.

✓ 14. It's easy for me to help people come up with solutions to their problems.

✗ ✓ 15. When my friends get down on themselves, I point out all their positive qualities to make them feel better.

___ 16. When a friend is bummed out, I'll bring over a funny movie and watch it with her.

✓ 17. I would go crazy without my friends to help me through every day.

✗ ___ 18. If somebody seems bothered by a comment I make, I try to explain myself better instead of just taking it back.

✗ ✓ 19. Before a test, people come to me and ask what I think will be on the test.

✓ 20. I'm always the first one to notice somebody's new haircut, shoes, or whatever.

___ 21. I'm totally not afraid of being the center of attention!

✗ ✓ 22. I can sense my friends' moods before they say a word.

✓ 23. I don't often give sarcastic answers.

X / 24. I have sports or hobbies that I do alone, even though my friends aren't into them.

+ / 25. If my friend volunteered to help at a recycling plant for the weekend and she needed help, I would go along to lend a hand.

SCORING:

In the following chart, circle all the statements you checked above.

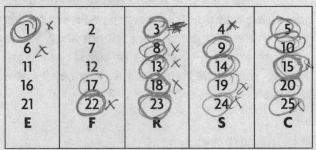

(1) X	2	(3)	4 X	(5)
6 X	7	(8) X	(9)	(10)
11	12	(13) X	(14)	(15) X
16	(17)	(18) X	(19) X	(20)
21	(22) X	(23)	(24) X	(25) X
E	**F**	**R**	**S**	**C**

Find the column in which you have the most numbers circled. See the letter at the bottom of that column? That's the scoring section you read below.

E Is for Entertainer

You love to: Make people have a good time.

Your ultimate hangout would be: Chilling with friends at the park and flirting with boys.

You hafta chill out when: Friends are in a mellow mood and don't feel like going out. A night of staying home alone doesn't make you a loser!

F Is for Feeler

You love to: Talk to your friends about your deepest, darkest thoughts.

Your ultimate hangout would be: A slumber party where you and your close friends play Truth or Dare (but mostly Truth) all night.

You hafta chill out when: You've been talking sooo long that you forget what you were talking about in the first place! Your friends know you're a sensitive chick — but don't be afraid to stop analyzing every little thing and just laugh every now and then.

R Is for Referee

You love to: Help everybody get along and be happy.

Your ultimate hangout would be: A day when all of your friends (even the ones who don't really dig each other) hang out in one big group and have a blast together.

You hafta chill out when: Two friends just don't get along. You can't force people to like each other. The best you can do is try to smooth things out, but then it's time to lay off!

S Is for Smarty

You love to: Push your friends to reach for the stars.

Your ultimate hangout would be: Cruising the coolest museums with your friends — no parents allowed!

You hafta chill out when: Your friends aren't ready to take big chances yet. Like, just because your bud says she'd like to be a dancer someday doesn't mean she's ready for a solo in the school talent show! Be supportive, not pushy.

C Is for Cheerleader

You love to: Help your friends realize how spectacular they really are.

Your ultimate hangout would be: A picnic where you can surprise all your friends by having their crushes show up!

You hafta chill out when: A friend has a real problem that can't be solved with a few compliments. Sometimes people need to feel bad for a while before they're ready to feel good. If you have a down-in-the-dumps bud who isn't responding to your awesome charm, maybe you should just let her cry on your shoulder instead of trying to cheer her up all the time!

Conclusion

The New You

By completing all the quizzes in this book, you've probably learned a lot about yourself. With what you've just discovered you can now take a step toward becoming the girl you've always wanted to be.

But don't just put down this book and go back to the way you were! Do something about it! Go back and find the quizzes in which you didn't score the way you wanted. Find the answers that belong to the girl you dream of being — maybe the one who's totally over shyness in chapter one . . . or the chick with healthy eating habits in chapter two . . . get the idea?

The rest is up to you. Start today. Push yourself and let your inner cool self break through!